Growing Tomatoes

An Essential Beginner's Guide on
Everything You Need to Know for Growing
Tomatoes at Home

David J Wilson

Table of Contents

Introduction 1

Chapter 1: Your Brief Introduction to Growing Tomatoes..........3

Chapter 2: Choosing Your Growing Spot.................................. 6

Chapter 3: Choosing Your Varieties.. 13

Chapter 4: Equipment.. 23

Chapter 5: Growing Tomatoes from Seed................................ 30

Chapter 6: Selecting a Seedling to Grow.................................37

Chapter 7: Getting the Seedlings Growing at Home 42

Chapter 8: Providing the Ideal Conditions............................... 51

Chapter 9: Maturing the Plants and Getting Them to Flower ..59

Chapter 10: Feeding and Getting the Tomatoes to Appear 64

Chapter 11: Understanding When the Tomatoes are ready to Harvest 72

Chapter 12: Dealing with Pests and Diseases 78

Chapter 13: Bringing Everything Together................................ 91

Introduction

When it comes to what fruit or vegetable plants to grow, there can be little doubt that tomatoes are one of the easiest and most popular out there. In fact, it's perfect even for beginners, and it is all thanks to the way in which they will effectively be able to grow themselves with little input from you.

However, that's not to say that you can just plant them and leave them to their own devices. Nothing could be further from the truth. The main thing is that you do not require any complex gardening knowledge or to be an experienced hand to achieve success. Just keep in mind that nothing in gardening is guaranteed as Mother Nature can always have a different plan.

So, what is this book all about?

Well, unsurprisingly, it's all about growing tomatoes and includes everything that you need to know about this plant from choosing the correct variety, to growing from seeds or plants, the conditions, pests and diseases, how to get the best crop and so much more. To be honest, there are a whole host of things to get through, but as we will continue to stress throughout this book, nothing is too difficult.

The amazing thing about growing tomatoes is that you can see the actual difference developing in the plants and when you see those first tomatoes starting to emerge from the flowers, there is a real sense of achievement and that you are well on the way to being able to enjoy that wonderful fresh taste.

Growing your own tomatoes is like nothing else. The taste, the smell, even the colour is different from those that you will purchase in a supermarket.

But here's the best thing. You don't even need to have a greenhouse in order to grow them. Instead, we will also take you through the process of growing miniature varieties indoors including telling you everything that you will need to then provide them with the perfect growing conditions.

Are you ready to go ahead and begin your education all about tomatoes? If so, then let's begin.

Chapter 1: Your Brief Introduction to Growing Tomatoes

To kick things off, I think it's best for me to really just give you a brief introduction to the entire idea of growing tomatoes.

I said at the start of the book that you can grow them either in your home or in a greenhouse, but I forgot to mention that, depending on where you live, the great outdoors is another alternative.

There is a huge array of tomato varieties that you can grow, and I'm talking about various colours, sizes, tastes and when they are going to ripen. If you thought that it was just red or yellow varieties, then you would be wrong. Instead, there are white, green, even tomatoes that are almost black in colour and then you have striped varieties as well.

Actually, some say that there are more than 25,000 varieties out there so at least there is a lot of scope and possibilities for you to work through.

Now, even though they may be in different shapes, sizes, and colour, that doesn't mean that they are going to prove to be any harder to grow. The truth is that everything stays the same no matter what.

Yes, there may be some variations between varieties when it comes to how often they need to be fed, and how much water to give them, but we are not talking about huge changes. By all accounts, anybody that is new to growing tomatoes should be able to select any variety they like, and they will still be able to succeed.

What I'm going to do in this book is walk you through each step of the process of growing tomatoes. I'm going to guide you towards the different varieties and how to choose the best one for your needs or preferences.

I will also look at teaching you how to grow from seed, if this is what you want to do, or how to nurture those plants that you will buy from a nursery where all of the initial hard work has been done for you.

I will also walk you through the way in which you will be able to get the plant to mature and grow, and the correct point where you can start to feed the plant to get the best tomatoes possible. In other words, by the time you have finished reading this book, you will have a complete understanding of what to do to grow amazing tomatoes.

You might also want to pay close attention to my chapter on pests and diseases as tomatoes do have a tendency to be attacked by all kinds of things. Also, the way in which you water them can have a major impact on the potential future success of your plants, as well as encouraging various diseases to hit the plant, so I will help you with that as well.

So, just to sum up this rather short first chapter, you might want to keep these points in mind as we prepare to launch ourselves into the real meat of growing tomatoes at home.

- Tomatoes can be grown by anybody.
- The conditions can vary a great deal making it easy to be a success.
- You can grow them either from seed or plants.
- You will learn how to mature the plants.
- You will learn how to water and feed them.
- You will learn how to get them to the harvesting stage.
- You will learn all about the pests and diseases that can cause havoc.
- You will learn how to enjoy your tomatoes and the varieties that you can grow.

I have a lot to get through at this point but I'm going to attempt to keep things as succinct as possible because there's nothing worse than a book just going on and on.

So, what am I going to do in order to get things started? Well, I need to really take it back to absolute basics and that is to do with knowing where you are even going to be growing your tomato plants in the first place.

Chapter 2: Choosing Your Growing Spot

The first thing that I need to discuss is the need for you to be aware of where you will be growing your tomato plants. This is more important than you realise simply because the space that you have available will also determine the variety that you can then grow.

Furthermore, some varieties are meant to be grown indoors while others are more for greenhouses and full on light, or even outside if your growing conditions allow them to survive.

It makes sense for you to know where you will have them or else you will be trying to grow plants in conditions that are just not suitable for them in the slightest, and they will not reward you accordingly.

So, what are your options as your growing spot?

Indoors

So let's say that you have decided to go ahead and grow tomatoes indoors. Clearly, you are going to have a number of things to think about because the varieties that are available for indoor growing are rather specific in what they need.

6

What you will often find is that they are not really that good at handling wild variations in temperature. This should influence where you will keep them indoors because if your tomato plants are chilled, and this can happen anywhere, then the growth will be stunted, and there is a higher chance of various diseases striking your plants.

However, the main issue for you to contend with has to be the light situation. Ideally, you would have a sun room or conservatory since there would be enough natural light coming into the space to help them to grow, but that's not always the case.

If you have neither of these things, then what do you do?

Well, you have a couple of options. First, you can at least choose the room that gets the most natural light for the longest period of time and keep it near the window. This can work, but there are a number of limitations associated with this.

The other option is to invest in some grow lights and they do not have to cost you a fortune either. You can go ahead and purchase LED lights but they are expensive and there's no need. Instead, halogen bulbs as grow lights will work just as well because the most important thing of all is that the plants themselves feel as if they are getting the correct light.

Of course, if you are growing your tomato plants indoors then you also have to think about the heat and how that affects the plant. You are best to only look at the dwarf varieties in this instance and then avoid them getting too much light or heat because that can lead to the plant stretching and have a negative impact on your yield.

So, for indoors I think you should be aware of these points:

- How much light will they get in this spot?
- What is the temperature like where they will be situated?
- Are there a number of cold draughts blowing through?
- How much space do they have without being too cramped?

As you can see, there aren't that many things to stop and think about, but they all play a role and are things you need to take into account.

Greenhouse

A greenhouse is the most common place for people to grow tomatoes and it's easy to understand why when you think about the setting. Not only can you regulate the temperature that the plants will be exposed to, but light should not be an issue either.

Now, there are various sizes available, and you don't need anything massive but this does depend on how many plants you plan on growing. There is not even any need for it to involve glass just as long as enough light can get through the plastic and that you are able to regulate the temperature inside the greenhouse.

However, just to make life that bit easier for you, I think that you should take some key points into consideration when you are either thinking about buying a greenhouse in the first place and also how to then grow your tomatoes.

- Make sure you give your tomato plants enough space.
- Remember that glass is not always necessary.
- Have the ability to control the temperature either hot or cold.
- You want to position it so it gets as much light as possible.
- Are you growing in containers, grow bags or in the ground?

There really is very little to worry about when you plan on growing tomatoes in greenhouses. In fact, the biggest issue is going to be the style of the greenhouse that grabs your attention and of course your budget, as everything else is pretty easy.

Outdoors

The third option is growing your tomato plants outdoors and this is something that is entirely possible pretty much no matter where you live.

The main point to remember with growing tomatoes outdoors is the climate. You will also have to make sure that they are planted in an area that gets the maximum amount of sun possible. The only other real piece of advice I'd give you with this is that if you do live in a place with a relatively short and poor summer, then go for the determinate varieties. This shortens the growing season so you have a better chance of actually getting something out of all the work at the end.

With the outdoors option, you also need to check the pH of your soil before you go planting your tomatoes into the ground. This will determine any feeding that should be included and also the balance of that fertilizer or you could easily end up with tomato plants lacking in some nutrients and overdosing in others.

The one thing that you cannot do is just throw your tomato plants into the soil at any point. The plants need to be firmly established and not too young or else any change in the temperature is going to often prove to be too much for them.

Hanging Baskets

The final option that I'd like to mention is the idea of hanging baskets as this can be overlooked and yet growing tomato plants in this way can be extremely satisfying. Now, it's obvious that you have to go for the dwarf cherry tomato varieties if you are growing them in this way since anything else will be too large.

Also, look for those that can also be trailing varieties although this does require you keeping a close eye on things so the trusses are not over laden and become too heavy. It won't take much for them to snap and break bringing your growing season to a premature end.

So, you have those different options and I've just offered a basic idea of what to expect with each one. There are a range of variations within each part that can influence where you end up growing your tomatoes.

The main point I'm making here is that you need to take time and really think about where you will be growing your tomato plants. You cannot just buy them, put them somewhere and then think about it. The last thing you want to be doing is shuttling your plants all over the place as they need to be settled into an environment for them to then be able to grow in the correct manner.

Now, I do get it if this sounds like comparing tomato plants to a new puppy that has to settle into its new surroundings, but too many fluctuations cause stress and no plant is going to grow well if it's under an extensive amount of stress.

But you will have hopefully picked up the idea that the actual location where you will be growing your plants is also dependent on the variety. So, that being said, I'm best to offer you some advice on choosing those varieties next.

Chapter 3: Choosing Your Varieties

Now, before I go ahead and start to teach you all about how to grow your tomatoes, we need to get one important thing out of the way, and that is choosing the varieties you will want to grow.

I hope that you've already made your decision as to where your tomato plants will be grown because, as I said in the previous chapter, this does have an impact on what you can grow.

In addition, the varieties and the location will also make a difference when it comes to the equipment that you need to have at hand in order to start growing your plants. Sound complicated? Well, it's not really as I'll now attempt to explain.

If you thought that it was just a case of selecting some tomato plants and that was it, then you are wrong. In fact, it's believed that there are somewhere in the region of 25,000 different varieties of tomato plants out there but clearly I'm not going to sit and go through all of them as I'd exhaust both you and myself.

However, I do need to clear up a few important points related to the different varieties. Believe me when I say that this is going to make your decision a whole lot easier than it would have otherwise been.

Heirloom Tomatoes

The first group I should mention are known as heirloom tomatoes. Basically, these varieties have been grown for an extended period of time resulting in generations of tomatoes. However, the key thing is that there has been no cross-breeding with other tomato varieties, so they are pretty pure, at least from a genetic point of view.

These tomatoes will often have a wide range of shades, sizes, and even patterns, and the fact that they are genetically pure does tend to mean that you will at least know what you are getting in advance. The taste and even how resilient they are can make your decision that bit easier.

Hybrid Tomatoes

Hybrid tomatoes are, as the name kind of hints at, the result of cross-breeding between two different varieties of tomatoes resulting in something that is a combination of both. Also, they tend to be the most widely available varieties out there and you will be able to spot them simply because garden centres have a tendency to write the word 'Hybrid' on the label.

Determinate Tomatoes

Now we are going to get into other aspects of varieties of tomatoes that you may have never heard of before and the first is known as determinate tomatoes. Varieties of this type will generally only produce fruit for a couple of weeks and then die off. It has a terminal growing point and will then go and grow flowers at that point, after which there is no more growth.

Indeterminate Tomatoes

Indeterminate tomatoes do not have that terminal growing point and will continue to reach for the sky until the frost strikes and the temperatures drop to a point where it just cannot live. It can potentially continue to produce fruit right up until that final point.

Shape of Tomatoes

Staying with the different varieties, there are some distinct references to the shape of tomatoes as being a way to determine various species (for use of a better word). Some of them you may already be familiar with.

- **Beefsteak** is one such variety and this is characterised by it producing the largest tomatoes.
- **Cherry** tomatoes are the smallest fruit, and will appear on dwarf varieties as well.
- **Globe** tomatoes are the most common variety that is grown around the world.

But here's the thing, I've not even got into different colours of tomatoes because that is yet another part that is worth exploring. However, you should already see that there are going to be far more options available to you when it comes to choosing the tomatoes that you would like to grow.

Things to Remember About the Varieties

I understand that it's all too easy for you to end up feeling rather confused and bewildered by the sheer number of varieties of tomato plants to check out. To be honest, I had no idea until relatively recently and I was taken aback as well.

It seems that there will be a tomato variety for pretty much any growing condition, but if you are indeed confused, then where do you begin?

Well, shortly I'm going to give you some additional information regarding some of the varieties out there to hopefully help you when it comes to making your decision. Before that, I just want to give you a few things to keep in mind when you then go on to read about them because I hope that by the end you feel better equipped than ever before to go ahead and buy the varieties that you would like to grow.

- Remember where you want to grow them.
- Remember if they are determinate or indeterminate.
- What size will they grow?
- Are they more resistant to disease?
- What size of tomatoes will you have?
- What do they taste like?

You see how I'm not talking about rocket science here but rather just a few pointers that should be in your mind as you make your decision. By all accounts, having these answers should make life easier and surely that's what we all want?

Choosing Your Varieties

As has been said several times in this chapter, I've only just brushed the surface of the different varieties that are out there, but how do you actually go about making your decision as to the ones that you should go ahead and grow? Well, I do believe that you should look at keeping these points in mind as much as possible.

At this point there are far too many varieties to list and we have already mentioned the most common varieties for the beginner, but at least giving you some extra information on the options and things to consider should make life easier.

The Ease of Growing

A key thing has to be the ease with which these tomato plants can be grown. This can be especially important for those individuals that are just starting out with growing tomato plants for the first time.

In my opinion, hybrid indeterminate varieties are the easiest, and here's another tip. Stick to either the red or yellow varieties at the outset because you will tend to be less stressed in trying to grow those varieties rather than wondering if the striped tomatoes are actually ready or when you should pick them.

To me, determinate plants with the shorter fruiting season can be stressful for the newbie. They will only produce tomatoes over a couple of weeks and there is more chance of things going wrong. I would stick to the hybrids in this instance.

The Crop

Some varieties of tomatoes are known for their ability to produce a heavier crop than others. Clearly, it makes sense for you to check out if the variety you are looking at falls into this category.

However, you also need to be honest with yourself. You need to be honest from the point of view of wondering as to whether you need a number of tomato plants that all produce a heavy crop if they aren't going to be used? Is there any point in doing that?

If you are planning on making sauces, chutneys, or other preserved tomato dishes then heavy cropping tomato plants would be ideal. Ask at the store you are buying the seeds or cuttings from if you are in doubt.

The Climate

As there are so many varieties, it's perhaps not a surprise that some will only be suited to a particular climate and this is something that you need to check out. Are you able to actually provide it with the growing conditions that it needs?

If you do live in a cold part of the world where you will struggle to provide your tomato plants with everything that they need over the period of several months, then in that instance I'd go with a determinate variety. By doing so, you will be able to focus your attention on getting the entire harvest over and done within a few weeks and not dragged on out until pretty much the first frost.

Resistant to Disease

Hybrid tomatoes are the best variety for resistance to disease. The very fact they have been bred together means they are taking the best bits of each variety and blending them together. This is mainly done to combat disease and other growing defects particular to a variety of pure tomato.

The Internet can be a useful tool and this is one point where it can be worth its weight in gold. You should check to see if you can uncover any kind of information regarding the main diseases that seem to affect tomato growers in your particular area before you buy any plants.

This can point you in the direction of varieties that are known to be more resistant to those diseases so you no longer have to worry about them being wiped out.

The Taste

I'm putting this part last in the chapter simply because I don't want it to get lost in the midst of everything else that I've said as it really is that important.

The taste can vary quite wildly between the different varieties with sweet and more savoury tastes being available. It makes sense to kind of have at least a rough idea as to what the variety in question tastes like before you invest your time and effort into getting them to grow.

Also, don't allow yourself to fall into the trap of believing that you will get a larger punch regarding the taste dependent on the size. It really doesn't work that way. Instead, you need to pay attention to the details that can be found on the label of the tomato plant that's for sale in the garden centres.

However, just to give you an idea of the difference, I want you to consider these points.

- The darker the variety, the more savoury the taste in most instances.
- The smaller cherry tomatoes will often be quite sweet.
- The variety of red, orange, and yellow tomatoes has smaller differences in taste.

- The actual height of the plant has no bearing.
- Providing your tomato plants with the correct growing conditions helps the taste.

As you can see, there's more to it than just thinking that a tomato looks nice and so you will then plant it up and watch it grow. You need to take every single point and consider them all simply because it does then go on and have an impact on your potential success.

There's also the option of just experimenting. If you go to specialist suppliers, and that's where the Internet can be your friend, then you can pick up all kinds of weird and wonderful tomatoes.

This includes some that have a range of shades all on the one tomato, others that are more oval in shape, white, almost black, pink, it's actually unbelievable the shades that are out there.

However, I would generally say that these rarer varieties are best to be grown later on and after you have gained some experience with the easier hybrid varieties that are out there.

Of course, choosing the varieties that you would like to grow is only part of the entire problem. You also need to be aware of the equipment you need as well as how to get the plants themselves to grow in the first place. However, I'm going to start covering those kinds of points next.

Chapter 4: Equipment

So, the intention of this chapter is to make sure that you have the correct equipment at hand for when you get to the point of being ready to start growing your tomatoes. Now the exact items that you need is going to depend on whether you are growing from seeds or plants that are already established as both have slightly different requirements at this stage.

Also, I want you to cast your mind back to the point where you decided on where you would be growing your tomatoes and also the varieties. Remember that some are dwarf plants and they obviously require different sized pots and support structures than other varieties that are larger. When you then throw in those plants that can be grown in hanging baskets, then you can understand why I'm structuring the book in this particular way.

Getting back to the equipment, I'm going to make life that bit easier by breaking it up into the different growing methods. Its then up to you to decide which one fits in with your preferred growing method but there will be some overlap between the different ways.

A Quick Check List

Now, here's the good part, you need very few items for growing tomatoes and that is always going to be a huge bonus to most people, particularly beginners. Also, it doesn't have to cost you a lot of money to get things started either, so there's no need for you to hang around any longer and wonder if it's all going to be worth it.

So, what do you need? Well, that's easy. Oh, I should also add that strictly speaking some of the items I'm going to discuss below are not actual 'equipment' but I do feel that they are important enough in the potential growth of your tomato plants for them to then be included.

Space. I talk about space at various points throughout the book as it does have an impact on things so you need to be absolutely certain that you have the space before you begin. For this, I recommend that you are aware of the varieties you would like to grow and how big they are going to be before you go ahead and make any kind of a decision.

Also, be sensible. It might seem like a good idea to grow as many tomato plants as possible, but can you actually manage to do this?

A Temperature Control. The temperature is important when trying to be a success at growing tomatoes so having a thermometer and, if required, a heater of some kind could be a good idea. I'll tell you later a bit more about the temperature requirements of your tomato plants, but as we are talking about equipment at this point I just need to stress that you have to be able to gauge the temperature or you will cause all sorts of problems.

Watering Equipment. Your tomato plants will need water, but I don't recommend that you just get a watering can and leave it at that. Instead, you should also have a mister or spray gun as well that allows you to control the force at which the water lands on the soil. Your tomato plants only require slightly damp soil at the start of their germination and soaking the soil is a bad thing and that's why you need the spray as well.

The Soil. Aside from the equipment, you also need to pay close attention to the soil that is going to serve you well for your tomato plants. Now, they are not any different to other plants in that they know what they like and will reward you in kind with a bountiful harvest.

For tomatoes, I always recommend that you use quality compost that is high in organic material. This is often going to provide more than enough nutrients for those seeds as they are trying to germinate, but I'll cover more about that later on in the book.

I also recommend that the soil is not too heavy. If it is, then it means the soil holds onto water for longer than you want and this can lead to all kinds of different diseases that can actually kill your plant.

If you do indeed end up purchasing soil that is heavy, then the best answer is to not throw it out, but to add some 10% vermiculite or even 30% of perlite to break it up. This will improve the drainage and lead to the roots not just sitting there saturated in water and rotting away.

But there are other things to take into consideration.

First, always use fresh compost with your tomato plants and especially if you are growing them from seed. Using what is effectively second-hand soil means it will have already been stripped of the nutrients that are in it naturally and that is going to get you nowhere.

You might also want to invest in a pH checker as well as having the ability to check the nitrogen levels in the soil throughout the growing process. Both of these can have a huge impact on the potential success of your plant and I will come back to these points later on.

So, what I'm really saying at this point is that you need quality organic compost that has nutrients and is free of microbes that are related to disease. It should be light and if you are concerned about it being too heavy then incorporate either vermiculite or perlite to help things along.

Having said all that a really good local garden centre will be able to advise you on the best products and they often sell speciality compost in bags just for the purpose of growing tomatoes.

Containers. With containers, you have a number of options available to you although you do need to take some care over the size of the container that you are looking at using.

If you are growing from seed, then a small pot or even a recycled yoghurt pot is going to be enough. If you buy a seedling from a garden centre, then the pot that it comes in is going to be large enough for the plant for a few weeks.

However, for the sake of the plant to be able to mature in the correct way, then you can use either a grow bag or a larger container that allows the roots of the plant to grow downwards and not to be too crushed.

The main thing is that if the container is terracotta, then the soil will dry out faster. If the container is plastic, then it will hold onto the water so making sure you do not over-water the plants is important as is good drainage.

In general the containers are going to be entirely your choice as pretty much anything can work. However, do note that you should only have one single tomato plant in a pot or it leads to all kinds of competition and the plants themselves will suffer as a result.

Other Items. There are various other items that I would certainly like to state that you should have just to make life easier. Also, the exact list itself is going to vary depending on the variety and size of the tomato plants that you will be growing.

For example, clearly if you are aiming to grow a variety that is in a hanging basket, which is quite popular, then you need the appropriate items. In this instance, you're looking at a hanging basket, a moss liner, and I would also recommend the self-watering variety as this does make life so much easier.

Alternatively, if you are growing the tomato plants inside your home and light is an issue, then you might want to go ahead and purchase some grow lights just so they get everything that they need to develop in the correct way. These vary in price depending on if you are using fluorescent lights or LED, but for the amateur grower just starting out, I would suggest stick with fluorescent lighting to keep the costs down.

Virtually any tomato plant is going to need support in some form due to the weight of the fruit. The best approach is garden twine and canes and I'll tell you how to set this all up in a later chapter. The cane should be around the same height as the fully grown tomato plant or else it could end up being rather top heavy and this will also be an issue.

Aside from that, a garden trowel and some specific tomato fertilizer are the only other things to concern yourself with. It really is as easy as that and you can see how the list of items that you need for growing tomatoes is not exactly extensive.

Chapter 5:
Growing Tomatoes from Seed

I'm going to spend this chapter talking about how to grow tomatoes from seed. If you have decided against this approach, then I'd just zip on past this chapter and go to the next one which I'm sure you will find to be far more useful.

Anyway, for those that have decided that they would like to try to grow from seed, then listen up. Growing tomatoes from seed is not going to be the easiest approach to take but that's not to say that it doesn't have its benefits. In fact, it does open up the possibility of you growing a greater number of varieties of tomato plants, so you could easily end up with something that's a bit different from the norm.

Now, the way in which you get those seeds to germinate is not going to differ with the variety. So, I advise you to follow these simple instructions for you to end up with a reasonable germination percentage.

Oh, I say reasonable because there's no guarantee that you will get a 100% success rate, so it's best to drop that idea from the outset because if it does happen, then it will be a pleasant surprise.

Since I have these kinds of formalities over and done with, let's get on with showing you how to get those tomatoes to grow from seed.

When to Sow the Seed?

The first point is knowing when to sow the seed. Generally speaking, if you are planning on always growing them indoors then it's a bit less of a hassle. However, the common approach is to look at the rough dates of when you can expect to have the last frost and when those colder nights have passed and then count backwards by a total of 6 weeks.

Now, that's just a rough guide but it should mean that you are not going to run into any problems with frost hitting your plants and stopping the growth in its tracks.

Getting the Container and Soil

At this point you don't want to put your seeds in a huge container as that will serve no purpose at all. Instead, even consider getting an old yoghurt pot and puncture a small hole in the base to act as drainage. Believe me when I say that this will be more than adequate.

What is more important is the potting soil that you use at this point as tomato seeds can be tough to germinate and you must provide them with as big a boost from the soil as possible. The soil has to be relatively light and not hold onto too much water. Also, it does need some fertilizer in it to really get things going, but not too much at this stage.

Starting with the Sowing

By now, I hope that you have the container ready and the potting soil already in it because you then have to think about sowing the seed and even with this there is some care attached to the approach you have to take.

The mistake that people tend to make here is that they believe that tomato seeds are like flower seeds that can just be scattered in any direction. Well, if you do believe that, then you're wrong.

Instead, you will get better results if you simply follow a few easy steps and surely since you want amazing tomato plants, then this is something you would want to do?

- **Step 1:** With your container, add the potting soil until it's close to the top but not quite full. Lightly tap the soil down to make it slightly more compact.

- **Step 2:** Add a little water to the soil so that it is just damp as the seeds prefer this kind of environment and it will make it easier for them to grow.
- **Step 3:** Make holes in the soil around ¼ inch deep. You can use a pencil to do this.
- **Step 4:** Gently drop a single seed into each hole and then pinch the hole closed.
- **Step 5:** Use a mister and dampen the top of the soil again.

The key is in just putting a single seed in a container (unless it's a huge container but that's not advised for the germination process) and you cannot just scatter them to all four corners. However, you are also unable to simply leave the seeds as they are after sowing them because to get the best results you have to push the germination process along.

Getting the Germination Going

If you just leave the container with the freshly sown seed in a greenhouse or in a warm room of your home, then it will start to germinate all on its own. However, we want to speed the process up somewhat rather than hanging around for any longer than we need to.

So, here's what you do.

The key is heat. The heat will help the seed to break through its protective shell and for the plant to then start to throw out its first shoots followed by it breaking through the surface of the soil.

With tomato seeds, they are going to really appreciate it if they are kept in a place where the temperature is anywhere between 70F and 75F. Now, that is quite precise in what they like, but it has been shown that this is the optimum temperature for getting things started.

I'm not saying that if you fail to have your containers at that kind of temperature that they won't germinate. They certainly will. The only problem is that it takes longer and the success rate might also be lower.

With this, you have a couple of options. First, you can buy a heat tray that sits under the containers. Next, you can buy grow lights that solve two issues at the same time thanks to the heat that is emitted from them. Finally, you can move them into a warmer part of your home where the heat is far more consistent.

Another key point is the water aspect. Some individuals will tell you that you should avoid giving seeds water at all, but I don' believe in that.

Instead, what I believe is that you should give them water although never soak them at any point. The soil should be kept moist and nothing more. I would also recommend that you use a spray rather than a watering can. For me, a watering can puts too much pressure on the soil and can potentially damage those fine shoots that are starting to poke their head through the soil.

Checking on the Seeds

The final points I'd like to make at this point is connected to the way in which you are able to check on the progress of the seeds. This is important as it can help you to determine if you need to perhaps increase the heat slightly to get things going or if the soil is too dry and it needs to be dampened slightly.

Now, I'm not saying that your seeds have to be checked on a daily basis, far from it but ignoring them is just not an option either.

To be honest, you should by all accounts start to see some progress and signs of life from anywhere between four to ten days after you sow the seeds. Of course, if you don't provide them with the heat that they need then this can be extended but generally speaking that is the time-scale you are looking at.

Oh, I also need to quickly mention something else and that is the issue of light. A number of people will want to put the seeds in a place where they can get light, but that's not important when you first sow them. Light only becomes an issue when the first signs of life are coming through the soil, so by all means prepare an area for them to go but don't stress at the start.

So, as you can see, dealing with the seeds and getting them to germinate is largely left up to nature with just a slight helping hand from your own self. However, just to recap on things, I strongly recommend you to keep these points in mind.

- Only make a small hole in the soil for each seed.
- Gently moisten the soil only and never soak it.
- Use a spray rather than a watering can.
- Remember the temperature should be between 70F and 75F.
- You should see results in anything between 4 and 10 days.

I do also get that some people that are new to this entire thing of growing plants at home may be slightly nervous but then the good news is that there is a second option. That second option is to purchase a seedling. However, even with this option there are various things that must be taken into account for you to then have some success at growing your tomato plants. So, I'll take you through that process now.

Chapter 6: Selecting a Seedling to Grow

A reasonable percentage of people are going to skip the seed germination process and go straight to a garden centre or nursery and buy a seedling. So, if you missed out the previous chapter, then welcome back.

Now, choosing this option will often limit the varieties that you have available to you, but that's not my main concern here. Instead, my main concern is in helping you to choose the best plant possible. I admit that this can be tough at times simply because some garden centres will tend to look after their young plants better than others and also the later into the growing season you go then the worse the plants look.

However, all of that can be avoided by you knowing what to look for. So, let's get to work on getting you through the process of initially selecting the best seedling for you to then grow.

Knowing What to Look for in a Seedling

When you venture into a garden centre that is selling seedlings, then you will tend to have a number of them to choose from. At first, you could feel slightly swamped by this especially if you have no real idea as to what you are looking for. However, it's easier than you may be aware and with so many stores selling them, then there's no way that you should end up with poor plants to go and start growing.

1. Check the variety. The first thing is to check the variety as there will often be several to choose from and you clearly want to get the right one for your needs. This is why I'm talking about this after my earlier discussion on the varieties simply because you need to know what to look out for before you spend any money. After all, you could easily end up with a beefsteak variety when you only have space for a cherry tomato variety and then what are you going to do?

Thankfully, they are usually pretty good at making sure that everything has a label and if you are unsure, then ask. The last thing you want is to get something that's not suitable and you only find out when it's not quite growing as you expected.

2. Check the base of the container. You will find that these tomato plants will come in small plastic pots and I advise you to look under the pot to get some kind of an idea about the root system. If the roots are really spilling out of the drainage holes and they appear like a matted mess, then put the tomato plant back down. It's going to be root bound in the pot and that can lead to all kinds of issues later on in the development of the plant.

In most occasions, you will want some roots to just be emerging through the drainage holes since it shows that the plant is well-established without having been in the wrong size of container for an extended period of time.

3. *Check the plant itself.* There are various parts of the plant that you should really be checking to make sure that you are buying something that is healthy and more likely to ultimately provide you with a healthy crop of tomatoes later on in the year.

Of course one of the first things is to look at whether or not the plant is withered in any way. It's amazing how often these places fail to adequately look after the health of their plants through poor watering. Now, finding a tomato plant that is quite dry might not be a lost cause, but it can lead to a whole host of diseases attacking it as the plant itself is quite weak.

With this, you will see the leaves have withered somewhat and curled up. They may even be turning brown and if this is the case, or even a shade of yellow, then I am telling you just to put the plant down even if they have reduced the price.

Another thing is to look at the height of the seedling. Now, clearly the further you go into the main tomato growing season then taller the plants will be, but what I'm talking about here is the space between the different branches on the plant.

If there is a large space between the branches, then it means that the plant has been forced on in its growth a bit too fast or else the branches would be closer together. Also, this can make the plant quite spindly and weak and the chances of you then having a tomato plant that gives you a good crop will have diminished.

4. Remember About Disease. Finally, you want to check for any signs of disease. Yes, this can still happen in a garden centre even though they should be throwing those plants out as soon as they spot that there is a problem. Examine the leaves, including on the underside, and if they are anything but a clean green, then put it back and even consider looking somewhere else for your plants.

As you can see, there are just a few things to look at when it comes to buying a seedling, but they are all very important points due to the way in which they can influence the potential outcome of your plant further down the line. Also, just one plant with a hint of disease could end up infecting the rest of your tomato plants at home, so it's just not worth taking the chance.

However, that is just to buy the seedling in the first place. You also need to be aware of how to help those seedlings grow when you get them home. The good news is that the growers have already done the hardest part for you, but that's not to say that it's impossible for you to then go ahead and make your own mistakes.

But, I'll help you to avoid those mistakes in the next chapter.

Chapter 7: Getting the Seedlings Growing at Home

I've decided to have a chapter on getting those seedlings to start growing at home because some people will make the mistake of getting the seedling and throwing it into a massive pot or grow bag right at the start.

This is wrong. In fact, it's very wrong and can easily lead to the plant being damaged and its growth either being stunted or stopping entirely.

The reason for this is simple. Transplanting a plant, especially a seedling, is traumatic for it. You stress it out and this can have a negative impact on it. You need to wait until it is at a certain stage before you think about moving it to its permanent home and I will cover that later on the chapter.

In the previous chapter, I spoke about the main things to look out for when you are buying a seedling in a garden centre, which is the most popular way of growing tomatoes, so I hope you've followed the points and are happy with the plants that you picked.

However, I said that you will still need some help in getting those plants to grow at home even though the germination process has been dealt with, but thankfully I'm not talking about anything too difficult.

The First Step

So, here's the first part. Let's just say that you went to your local garden centre and bought your seedlings and you are quite content with what you ended up buying. What now?

The one thing that you cannot do is just come home, throw them in their final pot and leave them in your greenhouse or the part of your home where they will be growing. They are not that tough at this stage.

Instead, you have to really break them into their new surroundings quite easily. I know this sounds as if I've lost the plot and treating them like a new puppy, but there are some important things to think about.

You must remember that they have probably been kept indoors at a garden centre as very few will have them sitting outside unless the weather is warm enough for them to cope. This means that they are not accustomed to the colder night temperatures, if you get them, and as the plants are very young and not hardy then this will be bad news.

The problem is if you get water on the leaves and then the temperature drops and they are sitting there in the cold. I'm not even talking about it being at freezing point or where frost can develop because the leaves can still end up being affected by the cold and the plant itself will be stressed. This, in turn, opens up the possibility of various diseases then being able to effectively get their foot in the door and that's something that you just don't want to happen.

So, what do you do?

Well, if you are planning on allowing the tomato plants to grow in your greenhouse, then I would recommend actually bringing them indoors for the first week or so especially if the temperature is going to drop significantly. Alternatively, you could purchase a heater for your greenhouse and have that on during the evening as this will help to keep the temperatures up enough to stop you having an issue.

The Second Step

The next step is to look at how to get the plants moving and growing because there are some rather specific steps that you need to take so that this part becomes as easy as possible. I'll go into the ideal growing conditions in the next chapter because they are so important that they deserve that time to themselves, but I'll include a few aspects here.

At this point, the plants should not exactly be in need of any feeding and you should also be careful with the watering aspect. The key is in providing them with enough light to encourage growth, but at the same time you want to keep them away from too much humidity and heat.

This will only lead to the plants being forced to grow too quickly and that is never a good thing. Slow and steady are certainly the way to go and the tomato plants themselves will reward you with a better crop later on.

The Third Step

One thing that you must avoid doing is waiting too long to move your plant to its final container leading to the roots getting crushed and the plant becoming pot bound. This can lead to all kinds of difficulties and the actual growth itself will be severely restricted.

Now, the moment where you have to transplant your tomato seedlings is up for debate. Some argue that you should do it relatively early on while others tell you to wait until several branches have started to appear. However, here are my thoughts.

If I was buying seedlings, or even I guess if I was doing it from seed, then I would avoid unsettling the young plant under two different circumstances. First, if there are no roots at all appearing through the drainage holes in the base of the container they are in. Secondly, if the plant is too thin at the stem and only has the first couple of branches as it will be far too weak.

So, let's say that there are a number of branches across the full height of the plant and it seems to be stable enough and strong enough to cope with the transplanting. At this point, you have to think carefully about what you will do next, but with the correct equipment and knowledge, then it should not prove to be that difficult.

How to Transplant Your Tomato Plants

These instructions only really apply if you are moving the plant into a larger container. If you plan on moving them into a grow bag, then you can just cut a hole in the bag, make a space for the plant, and then press your tomato plant into the soil. Add some water, and make sure your support cane is in place so that you have something to tie it to when it gets larger and requires some help.

Pots of various shapes and sizes are different. With a grow bag, pretty much everything is done for you in the way of preparation but pots will mean that you are forced into doing some of the work.

1. Get the container. The first part is to get the actual container and the size will depend on the variety. Clearly dwarf versions require less space than larger indeterminate varieties but even though the width of the pot is important, it is the depth that is actually the key.

This is because your tomato plants will like to push their roots down as far as they can go so you have to provide them with that space. Also, I do recommend terra cotta pots if possible. They allow air to circulate and get into the soil much easier and it will stop the soil from staying too wet as that will also be problematic for the roots. You should also avoid the glazed versions as the glaze can stop that circulation of air which is always going to be a bad thing.

Finally, you have to check that there are a number of drainage holes in the bottom or, as is the case with terra cotta, one large hole that will allow that excess water to escape.

2. Get the compost. The compost or potting mix if you would prefer to call it that is also going to be important so I should tell you what you need as this will really get your tomato plants off to a flying start in their new home.

Remember that they need something that has nutrients, but not too much because at this point they really are light feeders. To be honest, if you buy compost that states it has organic matter or fertilizer in it, then there's no need to add anything else.

3. Preparing the container. You should really add the compost to the container but make sure that it stops around half an inch above the top. Also, it may be an idea to sit the pot that your seedling is currently in inside the pot and then put the compost around it.

By doing so, you will be able to make the correct sized space for the seedling to go and it just makes life so much easier.

Once you've done that, gently tap or squeeze the sides of the pot containing the seedling and then give the pot a slight twist in your hand. This will help to loosen the seeding and root ball and allow it to then slide out of its old home without you damaging any of the roots.

After this, you should place the unearthed root ball and plant in the hole in the new container and then add some extra compost that is then firmed down around the plant. This should pretty much hold it in place.

4. The finishing touches. The finishing touches are very easy to do and yet they are also vital. No matter the variety you have gone for, you have to plan ahead and think about how you will support the plant as it grows and starts to develop the trusses that will hold the tomatoes.

For this, garden canes are the best option and I would strongly advise you to add the cane at this point so that you don't end up damaging the roots later on when the plant is more established. There's no need to tie the stem to the cane at this point as that can be done later but at least you are ready for it.

Apart from that, you just need to give the plant some water although that doesn't mean that you saturate it. Instead, merely dampen the roots and then move the container to where it's going to spend the rest of the year. It really is as easy as that.

Yet again, I seem to have covered quite a lot but there's still nothing too complex or anything that should stress you out. However, this is only part of the story because no matter the preparation up until this point, it all still rests on you being able to provide your tomato plants with the correct conditions that will allow them to grow.

So, perhaps that's where we should head next and I can guide you through the various conditions that you have to be aware of in order to get the best results from your tomato plants.

Chapter 8: Providing the Ideal Conditions

It will come as no surprise to learn that providing the ideal growing conditions for your tomato plants is going to be a no-brainer. Now, what those conditions will be is going to depend on where you are growing them, so I'll talk about each option individually.

This is also the point where your knowledge on the tomato variety that you are growing will prove to be rather useful. However, in most instances, things will stay pretty much the same across the board and this does make life a bit less stressful for you.

You may have already been able to guess that there are various key areas that we are going to look at in this chapter. Each part will have a profound impact on the ability of your tomato plants to not only grow and be healthy, but to then give you that fantastic crop of tomatoes after the flowering stage.

Now, I've said a number of times that I'm not going to talk about anything that is too complex or requiring specific gardening knowledge. Instead, this chapter is only going to stress the ease with which anybody can grow tomatoes even if they are completely new to growing any kind of plant.

Also, I could have gone into different growing mediums, mainly hydroponics, but that's getting more complex so I think that as this is aimed at beginners, then it's best to keep things nice and basic.

So, after that small explanation of my thought processes about this chapter, let's get going.

The Light

Any plant needs light in order to grow. Light is the equivalent of food for plants and your tomato plants are no exception to that rule.

In this instance, as the plant grows and moves closer to the flowering part of the process, you are looking at it requiring something in the region of 8 hours of quality light each and every day. Notice I said 'light' and clearly when you are growing them either outdoors or in a greenhouse then we are talking about sunlight.

Now, this doesn't mean that the sun has to shine 8 hours a day for months at a time for you to get amazing tomatoes. Just good strong natural light even if it is cloudy will suffice.

But what if you are growing them indoors? Well, if you are growing them in a conservatory, then you can see it as being just another type of greenhouse. However, if that's not the case in your instance, then at least keeping them by a window that is flooded with light is going to help. If that fails, then you may want to invest in some grow lights and I'm just talking about fluorescent bulbs and having them direct the light onto the plants.

Watering

Watering is where people often screw up with their tomato plants and that's because it is so easy to do.

The thought that comes into the head of most people that are new to growing tomatoes is that the more water you give them then the bigger the plant and the juicier the tomatoes. Well, if you give the plant too much water through the growing process, then you are going to drastically reduce the chances of you even getting a single tomato further down the line.

This is a real balancing act and it's one that you will undoubtedly get better at.

The watering situation is even more important when the plant is young as it doesn't need that much water. At this stage, it's all too easy to flood the plant and leave the roots saturated and that is just going to spell disaster.

At no point should you ever have the plant effectively sitting in water where it is unable to drain away thanks to the soil being so wet. Also, you need to remember that there has to be adequate drainage with the soil and that's why having the likes of perlite or vermiculite added to it is such a good idea.

The best approach is to adopt an even watering plan. This means you are going to water them on a regular basis and keep the soil moist. Note that I said moist and not soaked. Some people will water until they start to see some water coming out of the drainage holes and then stop and this is the guide that they follow.

Also, water the soil and not the plant. This is linked in with an attempt to limit the chances of you throwing up spores from all kinds of diseases that could be living in the soil and would then land on the actual plant itself. This can be the way in which these diseases really get into the plant and that in itself could prove be a disaster.

So, for watering do consider the following points:

- Never soak your plants on a regular basis.
- Tomato plants hate their feet being in constantly wet soil.
- Always water the soil rather than the plant itself to prevent disease.
- Give less water when the plant is a seedling.

The Temperature and Humidity

The temperature plays an important role in the ability of the plant to produce tomatoes because no plant likes there to be a wild fluctuation of temperatures at any point. This can have a profound impact on the potential crop you can then expect to have so it's best to keep on top of the temperature.

Basically, tomato plants are going to require somewhere in the region of three to four months of nice warm temperatures around the 70F to 75F on a daily basis to produce the best fruit. They can cope if temperatures go above that without any problems, but you then have to keep an eye on the watering aspect so that things don't dry out too quickly.

The temperature is important no matter the stage of growth that we are talking about here as is the humidity. If you are growing tomato plants in a greenhouse, then you need to allow air to circulate because too much humidity can cause problems. This is even more apparent in the early stages of the growth of the plant where too much heat can result in the plant growing faster than it really should and this just leads to a weak plant.

Fertilizer

I'll mention fertilizer at different points in the chapters that follow, but at this stage I do need to address one or two things since we are talking about providing the correct growing conditions.

Now, people think that tomato plants are going to require a lot of feeding because surely that is then going to lead to better tomatoes? Well, that's not strictly true and it helps if you know what to do in advance.

The first thing is you should really go out and buy a fertilizer that is specifically for tomatoes, and there are lots of different kinds out there on the market. These fertilizers have the correct balance between the levels of Nitrogen, Potassium, and Phosphorus that will lead to strong and healthy plants. This is better than just trying to use a general fertilizer and it's not even that expensive either.

Also, there's no need to give the plant some feeding in the early stages of its growth. The plant will be able to get virtually all of its nutrients from the soil and, once again, if you give it too much of the required nutrients, then the plant will actually suffer.

Tomato plants should only be fed when the flowers have appeared and the tomatoes are getting ready to burst from the centre of them. This is the key point and at that stage you should start to feed them once a week to then get the best possible results.

The Soil

I've mentioned the soil elsewhere already, but it's worth a quick recap at this point just to help refresh your memory.

Tomato plants love light soil with good drainage. It will lead to you getting the absolute best out of them. Also, the soil should be loose because it being compact is such a bad idea as that is when it will hold onto the water and cause problems with the roots.

There should also be a reasonable level of organic material in the soil as this will provide the young seedlings with enough nutrients to keep them going as they begin to mature.

Finally, I do need to stress that these things apply no matter where you are growing your tomato plants. They are the key ingredients that will hopefully boost your chances of having a successful crop, but prior to this you have to know how to get your plants to mature and even push them to the flowering stage. Believe me when I say that this is not a guaranteed thing unless you know what you are doing.

Chapter 9: Maturing the Plants and Getting Them to Flower

I need to stress the importance of this chapter because the way in which you get your tomato plants to mature and to the point of them bursting into flower will directly affect the kind of crop that you can get.

In addition, making mistakes at this stage can prove to be fatal for the plant and who wants to put in all of this effort only to go ahead and do that?

By this point, you will have moved your tomato plant over to its final home and it should have established its root system without too many problems. You should have also included the support stake while the plant is young or else you run the risk of damaging the root system and that would be a real shame.

Getting Your Tomato Plants to Mature

Growth is important. However, what is more vital is making sure that there is growth in the correct areas as you want your tomato plants to focus on developing into a strong plant and providing you with clusters of flowers and amazing tomatoes.

What it doesn't need is to expend some energy on those parts of the plant that are just going to serve no purpose. One such area is known as side-shoots which are additional branches that grow at the junction between a main branch and the main stem of the plant. In my opinion, you should remove them if you are growing an indeterminate variety of tomato. This makes the plant focus on the main plant as well as the trusses and it's those trusses that will give you the tomatoes.

To remove them, simply pinch them off with your fingers or use a gardening knife to cut them off at their base. Throw them away as they are going to be useless and there's no point in keeping them.

By doing this, you will basically be telling the tomato plant what you expect it to do when it comes to the actual growth part and it's amazing how it will then respond and effectively follow your instructions.

Keeping an Eye on Things

Now, you should be able to basically allow your tomato plants to grow their own way and without too much interference from your good self. However, that's not to say that you can just ignore them and watch from a distance.

Instead, your main concern has to be in looking out for a number of important points that can derail the potential growth of your tomato plants. These things include:

- Watching the temperature.
- Watching the humidity.
- Keeping an eye out for pests.
- Watching for disease and acting accordingly.
- Taking off those side shoots.
- Forgetting about feeding the plant at this point.

I'm really just talking about general care for the plants and you will then see that they will indeed grow just as long as they are getting everything that they need. This is perhaps the point where your research into the varieties that you are growing will make a difference as it just lowers the chances of anything going wrong.

This is the beauty of tomato plants in that there's no need for you to really do much at all although you have to be consistent in the things that you do. As you will see later on, erratic watering or temperatures can ultimately lead to all kinds of issues that you are best to avoid.

However, you will have noticed that I mentioned a need for you to avoid feeding the plant this point. I will also address when to do that in the next chapter.

Getting the Plant to Flower

Without flowers, you have no tomatoes. I will actually talk you through the process of getting those all-important tomatoes to appear later on, but at this point it's all about getting your tomato plants to that all important stage.

Here's the thing. The work that you have put into the growth of the plant and making sure it's in the correct conditions will now pay dividends for you since your plan will then reward you with flowers on the trusses.

However, you do need to keep a close eye on the nitrogen levels as that will either make or break the flowering process. Too much, and your plant will forget all about flowers and just reach for the sky. Too little, and it will just forget about growing completely and still no flowers.

At this point, I would also consider cutting out some of the lower branches because this will not only help to boost the flowering part of the process, but as I'll mention later, it also boosts the actual tomato production part as well.

So, to get your plant to the flowering stage, the main message I'd like to put across is simple. Slow and steady with the conditions. There really is nothing else for it and at least at the point of the flowers appearing, you can then gear up for giving the plant some much needed feeding so you can really boost those tomatoes.

Chapter 10: Feeding and Getting the Tomatoes to Appear

I now need to discuss the feeding of the plant and also how to not only get those tomatoes to start to emerge from within the flowers, but also how to get them to turn into fully-fledged tomatoes. Believe me when I say that this is not always that easy and there are a number of points where you could make mistakes that could spoil the harvest.

Feeding your tomatoes is important and you have to make sure that you are using the correct fertiliser in the correct amounts or else your tomato plants will not be happy. Well, when I say that, the plant itself could be happy but do it wrong and the plant will focus on growing the stems and leaves and forget all about the tomatoes themselves.

I mentioned in an earlier chapter that you should use a fertilizer that has been specifically formulated for tomatoes and that's something I stand by. You see, plants can be very specific in what they like and need in order to develop and tomato plants are no different.

There are two different trains of thought when it comes to the feeding of tomato plants. Some argue that you can give the plant some general plant feed when it's growing but only if it is well balanced. However, the problem here is that it is all too easy to actually over-feed your tomato plants and then you have a whole host of other issues to contend with.

The Soil

Now, there is something else that people will tend to overlook and that is the soil that the plants are in. If possible, check the pH of the soil or even look at getting your soil tested. This will tell you the levels of various nutrients in your soil and this could even then have an impact on the way in which you feed your plants and even how often.

However, if you are unable to get your soil tested, then the safest way to proceed is to just assume that it is balanced. This generally means that, in the earlier stages of the plant, a fertilizer that is higher in phosphorus would prove to be useful. Also, the nitrogen levels should be slightly lower as well.

Less Nitrogen is Important

You will often be told that nitrogen is the key ingredient if you are going to have amazing plants and, to a certain extent, that is true even in the case of tomatoes. The problem is that too much nitrogen can actually lead to your tomato plants just not producing flowers which then, as a result, mean that there will be no tomatoes.

So, here's what I recommend for you to do just to help improve the chances of you being quite happy with the crop that you can then have from your plants.

When you buy your seedlings, or if you grow from seed yourself, then give your plants a light feeding at that point. After that, you need to leave them alone and only water them up until the point where the first fruits are appearing. This is the point where you really should then switch to a fertilizer that is specifically for tomatoes since that will tend to be balanced for them resulting in the best outcome.

But this is another key point. Only add some fertilizer every week or two and no more than that. Also, never soak the plant with fertilizer as that is just going to cause all kinds of issues and it's something that you certainly wish to avoid.

Feeding Your Tomato Plants in the Correct Manner

I think it's worth me also pointing out how to feed your tomato plants in the correct manner because, let's be honest; you don't exactly want to make a mess of things, do you?

If I can maybe give a few examples to help you along your way. Let's presume that you are planting your seedlings. I would add some fertilizer into the potting mix and put this at the bottom. After that, you should then add some additional fertilizer on top, but make sure that this has not had anything added to it.

By doing this, the roots will be able to get the goodness as and when they need it, which is never going to be a bad thing.

However, I need to mention why the fertilizer in this instance should be mixed in with the soil. It's all to do with the way in which the neat fertilizer (which means it hasn't been watered down in any way) can basically burn the roots if it comes into direct contact with them.

Now, as you would expect, this is not going to be a good thing for the plants and yet so many people are oblivious to this being a potential issue and do it anyway.

Fertilizing with Tomatoes Present

I spoke about having to feed your tomato plants when the fruit is present but even with this, you have to be aware of the correct method or you run the risk of damaging your plant.

The fertilizer at this point still has to be watered down so it's not as strong as it is in the bottle. That is because the roots of the mature plant will quickly absorb the feeding and you will have effectively overfed your tomato plants and the roots will also burn due to the huge quantity of feeding that they have just absorbed.

As you can see, the key here is in how often you feed them and also the way in which you apply the fertilizer to the plant. Follow the instructions carefully when it comes to the quantities or you will be damaging the plant and all of the hard work that has gone into its growth beforehand.

Feeding is a key part of the growth of your tomato plants, so don't cut corners and follow the points that I have mentioned above and you really should not have too many issues.

Getting the Tomatoes to Appear on the Plant

The title of this chapter also mentioned a discussion regarding getting the actual tomatoes to go and appear on the plant in the first place. Now, so much of this will be down to nature, but clearly the way in which you deal with the conditions and care for the plant will also have a huge impact on this.

The most important part is in getting your tomato plants to flower since that's where the tomatoes themselves come from. This will mean that there are various ways in which the conditions can have a negative impact on the future production of those flowers and when you have a reduction in flower buds appearing, then clearly you have a reduction in the number of tomatoes that will grow.

I brought up the point of the importance of nitrogen earlier in this chapter, and this is certainly the best time to mention it once again. By all means, give your young tomato plants higher levels of nitrogen when they are younger, but when those buds are starting to appear on the trusses it's best to cut back on the nitrogen.

The reason for this is that your plants will just love the nitrogen and it keeps them nice and happy so they have no interest in pushing their energy towards flower and then tomato production. Instead, they are content to continue to focus on those lovely green leaves with your plants looking amazing. The only problem is that this is pointless since you will get no fruit at the end of it all.

It's also important to understand when the variety of tomato plant you are growing tends to harvest. Determinate plants will flower and produce fruit earlier than indeterminate due to the nature of their growth. Some tomato varieties just flower later on, so even if you fail to see buds appearing, you should perhaps not panic at first as it may not be a bad thing.

So, what do you do?

Well, that should be easy to work out. You immediately stop giving the plant nitrogen in any way, shape or form. Don't bother with trying to cut it down bit by bit as you will just be prolonging your own form of tomato agony, and why do that to yourself?

If you do want to feed your tomato plants, then switch to one that is noted for being higher in Potassium rather than anything else. This will help to kick the production of flowers and appearance of tomatoes into life, and that's what you want.

Another key thing to do is to start to remove some of the lower leaves and branches from the main stem. They are just using up energy and your tomato plant is just going to continue to let them grow unless you literally do nip that in the bud. You might also want to nip the growing tip out but this depends on the variety of tomato plant you are growing.

Those are the main reasons as to why your tomato plants may be struggling to get to the flowering part although if you are failing to provide them with the correct growing conditions in the first place, then clearly that will have an impact as well.

The thing to remember is that having no flowers earlier on in the growing season is not the end of the world. However, I do have to admit that if you are getting closer to when those first frosts are going to hit, then there's every chance that you will struggle to get any flowers appearing unless you are specifically growing your plants indoors.

Chapter 11: Understanding When the Tomatoes are ready to Harvest

Perhaps the most exciting time for anybody growing tomatoes is when you are ready to pick them as they have approached the harvesting period. However, some people mistakenly believe that you wait until they are a gorgeous red colour, or yellow if that's the variety, before you pick them, but that's not the case.

So, I'm going to guide you as to when to harvest your plant and also how to keep your plant going and tomatoes ripening even when the light source is fading due to the autumn fast approaching. There can be nothing more frustrating for the avid tomato grower than to have tomatoes that are just not changing colour due to insufficient light.

There are so many apparent 'methods' out there for knowing when tomatoes are ready to harvest. Some say that you must purely go on the shade of the tomato. Others say that if you try to pinch the tomato from the truss and it puts up some resistance, then it's not ready to be removed. Finally, some go for a squeezing method whereby they press the side of the tomato and if it fails to react and bounce back into shape, then it's best to wait a bit longer.

This all sounds rather fun but does it actually do anything? Well, that depends on what you believe. However, here's something that you may not be aware of and that is the simple fact that you can pick tomatoes from the plant before they are fully ripe so if you are unsure and want to take this approach, then you might not be so stressed out.

Now, getting your tomatoes to ripen can be done in two different ways, so obviously I'm going to discuss both and it's then up to you as to which option you prefer. I'm not saying one is better than the other as that's a personal preference and either will work.

Getting the Tomatoes to Ripen While on the Vine

The first approach is to get your tomatoes to ripen while the fruit is still on the vine. The key thing is that you have to change your approach to caring for the plant or else all of the energy will be put into the plant itself while you want the plant to turn its attention to the actual fruit.

1. Dealing with water. It's important that you cut back on the watering aspect and keep the plant drier than it has been up until this point. Cutting back on the watering actually forces the plant to go ahead and start the ripening process. You should also make sure that when you do give it some water that you only water the soil and don't put any water on the leaves.

2. *Remove leaves and branches*. Your tomatoes need light in order to ripen but often when your tomato plants get to this point they are covered in leaves and branches. What you have to do is to remove the lower branches and some of the leaves around the tomatoes themselves. By doing so, you will allow more light to the fruit helping them to ripen.

However, there's another benefit of taking this approach and it's also the fact that it stops the plant putting energy into growing leaves that just play no role in the overall success of the plant. You basically force more energy into the areas you want, which is always going to help.

3. *Remove the growing tip*. The thing about most varieties of tomato plants is that they will just keep on reaching for the stars and, of course, when they do that it does mean they are hardly going to be putting energy into ripening fruit. You need to look at the main stems and snip off the top of the plant. This is the growing tip and by doing this you will also force the plant to start investing its energy elsewhere.

4. Remove smaller tomatoes. When you look at the average tomato plant, then on most occasions it is going to be impossible for you to get every single tomato to ripen. Also, some of them are so small and insignificant that it's just not worth the effort. So, what I would do is remove some of those small ones as they are a waste of time and it then frees up more space for the larger tomatoes to grow and ripen.

5. Cover them at night. This is one thing that people virtually never do and that is covering their tomato plants at night. You could be forgiven for thinking that this would stop light getting in, but unless you sleep until 3pm then it's not going to be a problem.

The reason why you do this is that it helps to just keep the temperature up slightly around the plant and this can have a huge impact on its ability to ripen the fruit. Just remember to remove the covers in the morning or else you will have a completely different problem.

So, those are my five tips to help you with ripening your tomatoes when they are on the vine and I feel that so much of it is just common sense. However, I said that there were two methods and the second method is how to ripen them when they have been picked. Yes, I did say when they have been picked because tomatoes are amazing and the fruit will still ripen like this, so here are my tips to help you out.

Tips to Ripen Tomatoes after Being Picked

1. Get a jar. One method that I know has worked for a lot of people is known as the jar method. It's actually easier than you think because all you need is a glass jar, a ripe banana and some tomatoes. Place them all in the jar, a maximum of four tomatoes to allow space, and close the lid. Keep it in a warm place and by a marvel of nature the tomatoes will ripen.

2. Get a box. This is similar to the jar method, but you are pretty much swapping the jar for a cardboard box. Once again it involves a banana although I do recommend that you add in some newspaper to line the box. Place the tomatoes in the box and leave it in a warm place. You should see green tomatoes turn to their expected colour within 10 days.

3. Using a paper bag. Once again, I'm providing you with another different slant on the methods above, but I do have to stress that it needs a brown paper bag and I'd recommend swapping out the banana for an apple. Keep an eye on the rotting apple because this will inhibit the ripening of your tomatoes so it would need to be removed and replaced with another apple.

4. A sunny window. The final option I'm going to mention is using a sunny window. This will mean that the tomato will be able to get an adequate amount of light for it to ripen naturally and there's no need to cover it in paper or anything else. However, with this approach you will be best to rotate your tomato so each side can get enough light or you will end up with a tomato that is only ripe at one part.

There are several other methods for ripening tomatoes when they have already been picked, but for me these are the main ones and the ones that actually do work. As I said earlier, it's entirely up to you as to which option you choose, but at least now you have various things to think about.

For many, this is the part of the process that is the most annoying. There is just a sense of wanting to taste them and see if your tomatoes are as good as you hoped that they would be right from the beginning. However, patience is indeed a virtue and I would stress the need for you to just hold on and wait until they are fully ripe or you may be rather disappointed with the end result when there's actually no need.

Chapter 12:

Dealing with Pests and Diseases

Pests and diseases are the absolute bane of the life of the gardener and tomato plants are no exception to that rule. They do tend to attract a variety of problems at various stages of their growth cycle and even at the point where you are ready to pick your tomatoes only to discover that there is some kind of issue.

Now, how frustrating is that going to be?

The key, as always, is in being able to identify the problems as early as possible and I'm going to walk you through the main problems you need to be aware of and how to spot them. However, you will also learn about how to stop them in the first place and to deal with them to avoid you losing your plant completely.

With this, you could easily go out and purchase various sprays and pesticides to help you tackle the problem, but many people just don't want to go down that particular path, and who would blame them?

Think of it this way, would you rather use organic pesticides using natural approaches or those that are full of chemicals considering you will be hoping to eat the tomatoes? I know which one I would prefer, and I know that I feel safer knowing my tomato plants are not covered in chemicals. It may cost you slightly more for this option, but it's better to be safe than sorry.

Anyway, let's get into these nasty diseases and pests that you should be aware of.

How to Avoid Those Diseases?

I think it's worth my while just setting aside some time to really give you a few pointers on how to potentially avoid those diseases in the first place. As they say, prevention really is the best cure, and that certainly does apply even with tomato plants.

Now, I'm not saying that this is going to be fool-proof because diseases happen. However, there's no doubt that these tips will make a difference and at least reduce the chances of you being struck with diseases that could potentially wipe out your plants.

1. Check the Varieties. It's known within the tomato growing world that there are some varieties that are certainly far more resistant to disease than others. It makes so much sense for you to then go ahead and only purchase those varieties if that is indeed the case.

Remember I mentioned that there were hybrid varieties out there? Well, stick with those as they are certainly better at avoiding picking up all kinds of diseases.

2. *Check the Quality of Soil.* Often a number of diseases that affect tomato plants come from poor quality soil. Also, bad soil can contain the pathogens that lead to diseases, so I would recommend not scraping around for the cheapest soil you can find.

Also, you need to check things such as the pH and also add in some organic material to boost the nutrient content as this also leads to stronger plants and stronger plants tend to be healthier and more resistant to disease.

3. *Be Aware of Anything to do with Water.* With this, I'm talking about more than just the water that you put on the soil as it also involves the actual humidity levels as well. All of this can lead to fungus growing and if you usually water your tomato plants from a height, then stop it immediately.

The problem with watering in this way is that if there are fungal spores in the soil, then watering from a height means they can splash up and land on the leaves. This is the open door they have been looking for, and before you know it; your plant is covered in disease.

4. Avoid Cross-Contamination with the Tools. Tomato plants are quite fragile when it comes to disease, and that also includes cross-contamination from the tools that you use.

Look at it this way. If you have another plant elsewhere that has had an issue with a disease, then the spores of that disease could be on the shears you used to trim the plant. If you then go and use those same shears on parts of the tomato plants, then those spores can be attracted to the tomato plant.

For this, I do recommend that you make sure your tools are sterile and clean before you then use them on your tomato plants. However, this should be common practice for you, and by all accounts, you might want to do this after you have worked on your tomato plants just to get into the habit.

5. Deal with an Issue Immediately. Let me just paint a picture for you. Let's say you find that some leaves on a tomato plant are infected and not looking too healthy. So, what would you do?

Well, I'm telling you to act immediately and remove the infected leaves as this can sometimes stop the spread of a disease and prevent it from taking over your entire plant. Also, if a plant is infected with some of the more fatal diseases then take it out and burn it. Don't just throw it into the compost heap as the spores will live on. You also need to remove the container it was in and disinfect it.

6. *Consider Companion Planting.* I completely understand if you find yourself looking at this part and wondering what on earth companion planting is but the truth is that this can help to keep away various pests and it's all to do with certain plants being disliked by certain insects.

This might sound strange because, at first, you will wonder how one plant can help another in this way but it's not some strange magic as it has been proven time and time again.

The main things to consider planting alongside your tomatoes include the likes of:

- Borage
- Marigolds
- Basil
- Chives
- Nasturtiums

Often, they will keep away a variety of insects although I need to stress that this is not a cast-iron guarantee that everything will be fine. You just cannot assume that at any point but it has worked for a number of people, so there's no reason not to give it a go yourself even if you are growing them in pots or containers.

As I said at the outset of this section, I'm not saying that by doing these few simple things that there will be no problems with diseases. That is just impossible to state. However, if it can reduce the chances, then in my mind it's well worth doing it.

Common Pests and Diseases

This sub-section is clearly going to be very important as I'm going to quickly look at the most common pests and diseases that can affect your tomato plants.

1. Target Spot. This is when you see either brown or black spots appearing on the lower leaves. You need to remove the affected areas as soon as you spot it or else it will take over your plant and affect the chances of it maturing and developing tomatoes.

2. Fusarium Wilt. Fusarium wilt often starts with the leaves turning yellow and eventually wilting, working its way up the vine and the plant dying. It's more common in warmer temperatures over an extended period of time. You need to keep the pH of the soil around 6.5 to help combat the problem.

3. Verticillium Wilt. This is pretty much identical to fusarium wilt as it will also start in the lower leaves and lead to the death of the plant. Once again, you have to remove the infected parts as that are the only way to try to combat this particular disease.

4. Bacterial Wilt. If you get this, then throw away your entire plant as soon as possible. There's no other option. If you want to confirm if the spots you see on the leaves (as well as the yellowing) is bacterial wilt, then cut open a bit of the stem and put it in water. If you see this white substance coming out, then it's bacterial wilt.

5. Blossom End Rot. This appears on your actual tomatoes, and it spells disaster. This is not a disease as such but it's caused by poor calcium levels and you will often find that it's caused by lack of water or allowing the soil to dry out and then saturating it. This appears as a water soaked spot at the bottom of the fruit itself. The fruit will look soggy and rotten.

6. Late Blight. Late blight is caused by water spots that appear on the stem, the leaves and even the fruit. It's caused by spores landing on the plant and in the soil but you can counteract it by spraying your plant in order to protect it.

7. Cracks in the Fruit. There can be nothing worse than thinking that the tomatoes are perfect and you are close to picking them only to discover that there are cracks in the fruit. Once again, this is generally caused by you not watering the plants on a regular and consistent basis. The fruit will start to dry up then suddenly has a lot of water added to it which then makes it expand and this causes the cracks. At this point, you need to just throw away the tomatoes.

8. Aphids. Aphids can affect so many different plants, and tomato plants are no exception. You can spot them as they are small groups of small insects that often sit on the underside of leaves. They will eat away at the sap in the leaves but the good news is you can just blast them off with some soapy water.

9. Cutworms. Cutworms are pretty much like small caterpillars and they can do just as much damage. They have a tendency to attack the young stems and will do so at night when they will simply munch right through them. The best approach is to put a protective collar around the stems.

10. Hornworms. These are a type of caterpillar and they are pretty big at around three inches in length. They will eat away at the leaves but you can just pick them off and thanks to their size they are usually pretty easy to spot.

11. Nematodes. This is a horrible thing to have to deal with as these pests will attack the roots and kill your tomato plants in next to no time. However, not every species of nematode (there are apparently some 20,000) cause problems. Instead, only a few cause problems and they attack the roots making it difficult for them to absorb nutrients. This will lead to your plant struggling and basically dying.

Now, there are various other diseases and pests that are rarer, but the list above will tend to be the main ones that you could come across. As you can see, there is a mixture of those that will result in your plant being thrown out while others can often be prevented. However, early identification is absolute key and without that you will run the very real risk of losing your entire plant.

Chapter 13:
The Common Mistakes to Avoid

I admit that I've covered a lot of different things throughout this book, but I do feel it's important for me to take you through the most common mistakes that people tend to make when just starting out.

Now, don't worry if you do make them as you are not alone. It's how you recover from them and get your plants back on track that will prove to be the most important part.

I'm aware that there can be mistakes made at a range of points, so I think it's best to split it up into distinct categories just to make my own life easier in knowing what I've spoken about.

Mistakes, When Growing in Containers

Most people will grow tomatoes in a container of some kind, and there are various mistakes that are relatively common, and that can also have a major negative impact on your tomato plants. However, for me, these are the most common errors and how to avoid them in this instance.

The container is too small. A tomato plant is generally going to need the space for its root ball to grow and yet people will have a tendency to grow them in pots that are far too small. This crushes the roots, stops them from growing and both the plant and the potential yield is inhibited. If you're limited with space, then it's best to reduce the number of plants and have those you are keeping in large enough containers.

Over-watering. People think that as the tomatoes themselves are pretty much entirely water that it must mean the plant needs to be saturated with water on a constant basis because surely this would then lead to larger and juicier tomatoes?

Wrong.

Giving too much water and leaving the soil soaking is going to encourage disease to strike the plant and that can spoil the end of it all. If the roots are sitting in water, then you can pretty much drown your plant, and that's not a good thing at all.

Giving too little water. Yes, I'm well aware that this is going to really confuse the issue, but it's also possible to give too little water, and it's not uncommon for people to pretty much switch between the two as they try to overcompensate. Giving too little water is obviously going to lead to a whole different set of problems, but it still includes disease and the yield being restricted as well. The most common issue is blossom end rot, which I mentioned earlier, and as you know, this will lead to you having to throw the entire plant out.

You have temperature issues. Tomatoes love relatively constant temperatures, so having them fluctuating wildly and not counteracting this is going to be a problem. It stunts the growth so if you are keeping them indoors or in a greenhouse and the temperature is soaring and then falling at night, then you are going to get nowhere.

Instead, you have to regulate the temperature as best you can, so check it on a regular basis and use heaters if required at night.

Poor feeding. When you put compost in the container, you might be aware that there are certain levels of nutrients in the soil and some people think that this will be sufficient. Well, it's not.

I said earlier on that tomatoes are ravenous when it comes to feeding and if you are lazy with it, then those tomatoes are just not going to grow. Make sure that the soil you use has a slow-release fertilizer in it and also check you have a specific tomato feed, as I mentioned in a previous chapter, because feeding your tomatoes will lead to a better harvest.

The aim of this chapter has not been to try and put you off growing your own tomatoes at home because they truly are the ideal plants to grow even for individuals that are new to gardening in general. However, each point that has been mentioned in this chapter is very important. It's important.

And remember this important point; it's only a plant at the end of the day. Dont beat yourself up too much if you fail a few times at first. Just roll your sleeves up and move on to the next one till you get it right, and believe me with practice you will get it right.

Chapter 13: Bringing Everything Together

My final chapter is really just a summary of the things I've spoken about and to really provide you with some kind of a snapshot of the key points that should help to just propel you forward with your tomato growing experience. Remember, it's impossible to completely predict how successful you are going to be because sometimes Mother Nature and the plants themselves just seem to work against you no matter how hard you try.

I hope I've managed to put across the idea that tomato plants can be fun to grow and with so many options out there, it really should be an easy enough case to find something that fits in with your own personal preferences.

Also, you will have perhaps noticed that there's not even a real need for you to have all kinds of equipment and gardening knowledge to be a success at growing tomato plants. I like to believe that this is one of the main reasons as to why it's so popular.

Basically, you just need the following things, and you can get started:

- Some space in your home.
- A pot large enough for a mature tomato plant.
- A cane to give support.
- Some garden twine.
- Something to add water to soil.
- Tomato feeding.
- A tomato plant.
- A light source of some kind.

Now, please note how I never mentioned anything that is too expensive. I just don't believe in people starting out with growing something and spending a fortune to do so. I always feel it's best for you to get a sample of what it's like to grow tomato plants and how easy it can be before you start investing your hard-earned cash in additional equipment.

Once you have cracked the tomato growing process then by all means start investing in more expensive equipment.

But let me just run through the different chapters and offer you a summary of the key points. Look at this chapter as pretty much being the sort version of the book, although I would stress that it can certainly be worth your while going back to the relevant chapters.

Choosing Your Spot

Choosing your spot was the first thing that we looked at, and it's easy to understand why. The location where your tomatoes will be grown will have a direct impact on the varieties that you will be able to choose from. After all, there's no point in growing large plants in a confined space. It's just not possible.

However, the main things to take away from that particular chapter include:

- Being aware of the conditions that will be present in the growing spot.
- Being aware of the space that is available and how many plants you can grow.
- Understanding how conditions can fluctuate in the area.
- Being aware of the varieties that can grow in that spot.

Choosing the Varieties

In my chapter on choosing the varieties, I went through the different types of tomatoes that are out there on the market, but effectively left it up to you to ultimately decide on the names that you should grow. For me, this was important because it's impossible for me to know the conditions you will be growing them in, so to go and prompt you into choosing certain names would be madness.

That being said, I do feel you should keep these points in mind:

- Heirloom tomatoes have no cross-breeding.
- Hybrid tomatoes have been cross-bred.
- Determinate tomatoes produce fruit over just a few weeks.
- Indeterminate tomatoes will produce fruit until the last frost.
- There are various shades of tomatoes available as well as size.
- Often, the darker the shade, the more savoury it tastes.
- Be aware of how heavy the crop is for a variety and how it fits into the growing space.

Your Equipment

The main point I was trying to make when it came to the equipment side of things was that there's no need for you to have a lot of different items to grow tomatoes. Forget the idea that you need a greenhouse as growing them indoors or even in a hanging basket is always an option. Equipment can be basic because tomato plants are just that, quite basic and do require very little gardening knowledge for you to be a success.

or me, the main items you need to remember when it comes to equipment include:

- A container or grow bag to grow your tomatoes.
- A watering can.
- Some organic fertilizer.
- Some compost.
- The ability to know the temperature.
- A cane and twine for support.
- A source of light if you are growing them indoors.

Growing from Seed

I feel that only some people will have read and concentrated on my chapter regarding growing from seed, but that's fine by me. I am aware that if you are new to all of this, then the idea of trying to get a plant to germinate when you can go ahead and buy a seedling would seem to be slightly alien to a lot of people.

However, for those people that are interested in giving this a go, then I would recommend these key points for you to remember:

- Choose your seeds wisely.
- Use small pots with drainage holes.

- Use potting compost with organic material for feeding.
- Lightly water.
- Only put one seed in the pot and half an inch into the soil.
- Add some heat and forget about light.
- You should see life within 10 days.

Choosing a Seedling to Grow

Now, if you have gone for the second option, then this was an important chapter since I took you through how to choose a seedling from a garden centre. Unfortunately, not every garden centre is going to take care of its seedlings, and that's why you need to pay attention to what you are buying.

For that very reason, I brought up a number of key points that should, at least, make things a little bit easier for you:

- Check the roots to see if they are coming through the pot.
- Check the spacing between branches to see if it has been forced to grow.
- Look for any signs of disease.
- Check if it has been watered.
- Check the variety and ask about it if unsure.

Getting the Seedlings to Grow

It made sense to move onto helping you to get the seedlings to actually grow when you get them home because this is also a point where people can go wrong and start to make a number of mistakes. However, I've hopefully shown you that it really does not have to be that difficult if you just follow a series of key points.

So, in this instance, I think that you should really remember these things to help you out:

- Never transplant the seedling into another container straight away.
- Be aware of temperatures at night and bring it indoors if required.
- Wait until the seedling is strong enough before you think about transplanting.
- Avoid giving it any feeding as the soil it's in should suffice.
- Be constant with the watering and keep it light.
- Follow my simple steps for transplanting into the preferred container.

The Ideal Conditions

I had mentioned the ideal conditions on a number of occasions before this point, so it made sense to dedicate an entire chapter to it since it does have a profound impact on the future success of your plants. In this instance, I covered everything that you would want to know regarding the conditions that your tomato plants will thrive in, and I do believe that there was nothing too taxing in there.

However, as a reminder, these points stand out for me.

- Make sure that the soil is well-drained and light.
- Keep the soil wet but not saturated.
- They need around 6 to 8 hours of light per day.
- They need temperatures during the day between 70F and 75F.
- Feeding only happens early on and when the tomatoes are starting to appear.

To be honest, there are plants out there that need a lot more care and attention than this, which is why I love growing tomato plants in the first place.

Getting the Plants to Mature

Getting the plants to mature is important since it then has a direct impact on the ability of your tomato plants to then produce the fruit at the end of it all. What I tried to show was that you don't really have to stress that much over the plants at this stage, although there are one or two things that you can do that will help the plants really move along.

That being said, perhaps keep these points in mind:

- Be constant with the watering, temperature, and light.
- Keep an eye out for disease and react immediately.
- Avoid giving the plant too much nitrogen.
- Remove lower branches to push the energy into the flowering.

Getting the Tomatoes to Appear

If you have got to the point where the plant has matured, and flowers have appeared, then this chapter had the intention of helping you to get those tomatoes start to emerge from the flowers. This was all about changing the way in which the plants are fed and increasing potassium just to help things along. However, I also gave a warning about the watering once again as this can lead to problems.

- Start feeding with a balanced feed or one high in potassium.
- Feed once a week and read the instructions.
- Remove excess foliage to give space for the tomatoes.
- Water in a constant manner to stop issues with the tomatoes.

Getting them Ready to Harvest

This was one of the happier chapters since it dealt with the issue of knowing when your tomatoes are actually ready to be harvested. My main concern here is you not having the patience to allow nature to take its course, which is why I looked at providing you with some tips on helping your tomatoes to ripen.

- You can ripen either on the vine or off them.
- Learn the tips to know when they are ready for harvesting.
- Pinch, twist, and shade, are key.
- Remember the bag, box, and jar method for ripening off the stem.

Dealing with Pests and Diseases

Pest and diseases are a pain, but then every plant is affected by them, so tomatoes are no exception. I didn't give a complete list of issues, but I did focus on the main ones that most people will complain about. Keeping a close eye on things is certainly the way to go although I did offer some additional advice to make life easier for you.

- You cannot guarantee prevention.
- Pests and diseases should be treated with organic items.
- Not all diseases spell the end of the plant.
- Fast action is key to stop it spreading.
- Be aware of those diseases that should result in your plant being thrown out.

Common Mistakes to Avoid

Finally, I looked at the common mistakes that people tend to make when growing tomatoes in the hope that you would then know how to avoid them. Now, everybody makes mistakes, so it's best to just accept that simple fact and get on with it. However, I feel that you can still learn from this chapter and at least reduce the chances of you making a huge error.

- Keep an eye on the conditions.
- Keep an eye on the plants you buy in the first place.
- Be patient with your plants.
- Only grow the correct varieties for your space.

The best part of all is that tomato plants reward you when you do things right. It's just up to you to put the various tips and advice mentioned above to good use, and hopefully, you will then be given some amazing tomatoes to enjoy at home.

Despite all the warnings and advice please enjoy being a tomato gardener. The experience is a wonderful one of producing food from seed to plate. Make mistakes, it makes us better gardeners after all!

But above all HAVE FUN!!